6-8

422
N

C.1

NURNBERG, MAXWELL

WONDERS IN WORDS

© THE BAKER & TAYLOR CO.

WONDERS IN WORDS

By Maxwell Nurnberg

Illustrated by Fred Turton

PRENTICE-HALL, INC., ENGLEWOOD CLIFFS, N.J.

WONDERS IN WORDS by Maxwell Nurnberg
© 1968 by Maxwell Nurnberg

Library of Congress Catalog Card Number: 68-15761
Printed in the United States of America   ●   J
Prentice-Hall International, Inc., London
Prentice-Hall of Australia, Pty. Ltd., Sydney
Prentice-Hall of Canada, Ltd., Toronto
Prentice-Hall of India Private Ltd., New Delhi
Prentice-Hall of Japan, Inc., Tokyo

To Rose and Ellen,
who share with me the fascination of words

Contents

How long a time lies in one little word!

WILLIAM SHAKESPEARE: *King Richard II*

. 1 .

THE MYSTERY AND
WONDER OF WORDS

Millions of years ago, there were no words. There was
no language. The first human beings, like animals,
were probably able to make only those sounds that
expressed the simplest feelings. They must have made
sounds like the bark of a dog to convey excitement or
like the purr of a cat to show contentment. Man was
very much like Tennyson's

> An infant crying in the night;
> An infant crying for the light,
> And with no language but a cry.

These sounds and cries nature gave to man as she
gave him hands. Man's hands, however, were not by
themselves powerful enough to conquer the earth and
get from it everything that was needed. Therefore, he
had to invent tools made out of wood and stone to
extend the power of his hands.

In the same way man had somehow to create or
invent **words, tools made from sounds**, to extend
his power of communication with others, to share with
them some of the ideas that lay imprisoned in his brain.

One day, aeons ago, it is possible that an early
ancestor of ours, running barefoot on the forest floor,

1

suddenly happened to step on a sharp stone. Un-
doubtedly he uttered a startled, piercing cry of pain—
the primitive equivalent of a word like "Ouch!" He
was probably frightened by his outburst, yet somehow
excited by it too.

Imagine him later that day back in his cave. Remem-
bering the sharpness of the pain, he was eager to let the
others know all about his experience. As he acted out
his story for them with gestures, he came to his startled
outcry. Having a sense of the dramatic, he pointed to
the sole of his injured foot and, to make his story more
vivid, let out the same piercing sound he had made at
the time of his accident.

The story was an instant success. He was made to
tell it over and over again, the others joining in when he

came to the "sound effect." After frequent repetitions we can see how the sound became a word that they could now all use. And it probably had many meanings. Depending on the particular gesture that accompanied it, the word could mean *pain* or *wound* or *blood* or *sharp stone* or even *sole of a foot!*

How do we know all this? We don't. Through the years, students of language have developed many theories, pure guesses. This is my guess.

However, at this point science can step in to help us with part of the story of language. For there is a theory which says, "Ontogeny recapitulates phylogeny." Simply stated, it tells us that the individual, especially in his earliest stages, goes through a development similar to those stages that the human race has gone through. If, therefore, we study how a little child's language develops, it may give us some idea of how language itself developed.

Let us take the case of Ellen. She was a big-city child, surrounded constantly by passing automobiles and trucks. Therefore, the first word she learned—it was really a sentence—was "It's a car." She would call attention to each passing vehicle proudly with "It's a car."

On her first day in the country, she saw an ant crawl by. Her pudgy little finger shot out and triumphantly she announced, "It's a car." For Ellen, anything that moved was a car. No distinctions or refinements were made. *It's-a-car* was a general word to describe any moving object.

In the same way, the "ouch" word of our earliest ancestors was a general word and often covered a lot of ground. Later, much later, more specific words were developed. *Ouch* remained the word for a cry of pain and other words were found for *stone* and *sharp* and *pain* and *wound* and *blood* and *sole* that had specific, unique meanings. Today, Webster's Third New International Dictionary contains 450,000 separate entries. And there exist in the world today about 2,500 languages!

In his play *Prometheus Bound*, Robert Lowell has Prometheus say:

"Before I made men talk and write with words, knowledge dropped like a dry stick into the fire of their memories, fed that fading blaze an instant, then died without leaving an ash behind."

It is written words that have made man's memories live on in others and have fed the flame of knowledge which lighted the avenues to all of man's serious thinking and his great achievements.

For example, you press a button and where there was darkness before there is now light. You press another button and you shoot up eighty floors, almost to the top of the Empire State Building. You turn a dial in your living room and you are present at an event taking place thousands of miles away. These miracles, which have taken millions of years to achieve, are taken for granted by all of us.

In the same way, we take for granted another miracle—the words we speak, read, and write so naturally and effortlessly. Let's take a very simple example. Every morning, wherever English is spoken, people sit down to what they call *breakfast*. Few of us ever think of the word as meaning more than merely some fruit juice, a cereal or egg, toast, and a hot drink. Yet if you look closely at the word, you see that it means that you are *breaking* your *fast*, eating for the first time since the evening before.

You *don* (do on) your clothes before sitting down to breakfast and you may *doff* (do off) your hat when you say goodbye. But what are you saying when you say goodbye? In Shakespeare's plays you will find that characters, on leaving one another, sometimes say, "God be wi' ye!" (God be with you!) Now say *God be wi' ye* fast. Faster. Faster still. In a few seconds you have covered hundreds of years and you have arrived at the modern *goodbye*. Thus whenever you say goodbye you are really saying, "God be with you."

In most modern languages of Western Europe the formal words of farewell have God in them. The French say "Adieu"; so do the Germans and Austrians though they pronounce it a little differently. The Spaniards say, "Adios" and the Italians, "Addio." All of these words come from the Latin word for a god, *deus*, which comes from the Greek *theos*, which comes from—but that's another story and another book.

You may eat breakfast with, or say goodbye to, a *companion*. Let's not take that word for granted. Let's look into it. *Companion* has the structure of most English words of three syllables or more: a prefix, *com*; a root, *pan**; a suffix, *ion*.

You have seen the prefix *com* in words like *combine, combat* (fight *with*), *compose* (put *together*), and you probably know that *com* is a prefix meaning "with" or "together." The suffix *ion* shows that the word is a noun.

But what does the all-important middle part **pan** mean? It comes from a Latin word *panis*, appearing in French as *pain* (pronounced "paa" with a nasal twist at the end), in Spanish as *pan*, and in Italian as *pane* (pronounced "pah-nay") and it means bread. Is there a better way to describe a companion than to say that he is one with whom we share our bread?

You probably know that the word *alphabet* is made up of the first two Greek letters—*alpha* and *beta*. But do you know that the word *atone* really means *at one*? If you *atone*, if you make amends, for something you

---

*In more technical books, distinctions are sometimes made between roots and stems, combining forms and elements. We're going to simplify things by using the word **root** for any part of a word that isn't *ordinarily* used as a prefix or suffix. The ordinary **prefixes** are the familiar syllables *ab*, *ad*, *anti*, *dis*, *ex*, *per*, *pro*, etc. that come at the beginnings of words and often influence their meaning greatly. The ordinary **suffixes** are the familiar *ance*, *ous*, *ence*, *ent*, *ive*, *ion*, *ize*, *ly*, *ment*, etc. that come at the end of a word and often merely determine whether the word is a noun, a verb, an adjective, or an adverb.

have done, you feel *at one* again with man and God. Do you know why a word coming from the moon means insanity? Do you know why *tragedy* means a goat song? Do you know why *lb.* means pound?

If all you know about a word is its spelling and its meaning, you sometimes don't know the half of it. As a matter of fact, you don't know the most interesting half of it. You don't know who its parents are, who its relatives are, what country it was born in, or what picture may be hidden somewhere within it.

In the pages that follow we're going to try to get behind and inside words to find out something about their ancestors, about a once vivid picture they may have presented, and anything else that may be unusual or interesting about them. We're going to be "logonauts,"* sailors among words, to explore some of their wonder and magic, and to try to reveal what goes on inside. To *reveal* is to draw back (*re*) the *veil*!

By the way, the word *infant* comes from Latin *in*, not, plus *fant*, speaking. Strictly speaking, therefore, you are no longer an infant when you begin to speak.

---

*This shows how easy it is to coin or make up new words. You just take two old words—in this case Greek *nautes* (root *naut*), "a sailor," and *logos* (root *log*, *logue*), "word,"—and put them together. Such newly coined words are called *neologisms* (*neo*, new, + *log*, word, + suffix *ism*).

2

WORDS RIGHT OFF
THE MAP

Television in its news coverage has brought the whole world into your living room. Cities, towns, and even countries you may never have heard of before suddenly become part of your everyday conversation.

However, your daily conversation—without your always knowing it—has often contained words that came to us right off the map. Some are as easy to see through as **china** and **vichy**. Others need a closer look to discover their geographical connection.

In fact, man could get along pretty well if he were limited to the use of only those things that have come right off the map. We could dress him from head to toe. On his feet? **Oxfords** (England). On his head? He'd have a choice. He could wear a **derby** (England again), though the equivalent English hat is called a bowler. Or a **homburg** (Homburg, a fashionable health resort in Germany where these black felt hats were first worn). In summer, of course, he could wear a **Panama** (formerly the chief distribution point, though the hats are actually made in Equador).

If he felt like going riding, he could wear **jodhpurs** (Jodhpur, the capital city of a province in India) and a jersey (the largest of the Channel Islands off Normandy).

If he wished to be more formal, he could wear a *tuxedo*, which gets its name from Tuxedo Park, New York. In 1866, at a ball given in celebration of the opening of the exclusive men's club there, Pierre Lorillard, defying convention, appeared in a suit he had had tailored in England. It was a full-dress suit without swallowtails. One of the Astors who was present appropriately named it a "tuxedo."

If, in this formal mood, our geographical hero wanted to take his best girl out for a drive, he would use either a *coach* (Kocs, a village in Hungary near Budapest) or a **surrey**, with or without a fringe. Though the surrey is as American as the operetta *Oklahoma!*, the four-wheeled pleasure cart was first built in the county of Surrey, England, and introduced into this country in 1872.

He couldn't hitch up any "high-stepping strutters"; he'd have to be satisfied with **Percherons** (from La Perche, the district in France where these powerful horses are raised). Perhaps he wouldn't feel so bad about using horses that in modern times are employed for hard labor, if he knew that in the Middle Ages they were the only horses strong enough to carry knights in full armor. The gait our young man could drive his horses at would be a **canter** (from Canterbury, England, describing the easy trot of Chaucer's Canterbury pilgrims as they jogged along).

What kind of evening would our map-bound young man spend? Well, he could take his girl to dinner, limited in choices to be sure, and the menu would be printed in **italics** (from Italy, where in 1501 the famous printer Aldus Manutius first used the slanting type). Our couple would have dinner served on delicate *china*, of course, and cooked in pots of *copper* (a word that comes from *Cyprus*, an island where copper was plentiful). They would have a choice of the following:

APPETIZERS: **cantaloupe** (from the castle of Cantalupo, Italy, formerly the Pope's country home, where these melons were first cultivated in the sixteenth century from seeds brought from the Near East); **sardines** (from the island of Sardinia); and **baloney**, or **bologna**, from Bologna (a large city in northern Italy).

MEATS: **hamburgers** (originally called hamburger steaks from Hamburg, Germany); **frankfurters** (first called Frankfurter *wursts* or sausage from Frankfurt, Germany); and, of course, **turkey**, though no one is quite sure why the popular bird was given this name.

DESSERTS: **tangerines** (from Tangier, Morocco); **currants** (raisins of Corinth, Greece); **peaches** (Persian apples, through Latin *Persicum malum*); and a choice of cheeses: **cheddar** (England); **gruyere** (Gruyere, Switzerland); **camembert**, or **roquefort** (cities in France); **parmesan** (Parma, Italy); and **limburger** (Limburg, Belgium).

BEVERAGES: **cognac** (France); **champagne** (France); **port** (Oporto, Portugal); **vichy** (France); **seltzer** (Selters, Germany); or **sherry** (from Jerez, Spain, pronounced *sherris* in sixteenth-century England, the final *s* later dropped because people mistakenly thought that the word *sherris* was a plural form).

Conversation during the meal? Yes. He might resort to **blarney** (a village near Cork, Eire) which means smooth, flattering talk; or he might tell her about his college days when he starred at **badminton** (the name of the Duke of Beaufort's estate in England) and **rugby**, a game originally played at Rugby School, Rugby, England. He might even boast of his great skill in the use of such weapons as the **bayonet** (Bayonne, France, where the short blades were first made) and the **shillelagh** (pronounced shill-ay-lee, coming from Shillelagh, Eire, famous for its oaks).

And nobody would blame the young lady if she thought it was all the **bunk** (abbreviation of *bunkum* from Buncombe County, North Carolina).

After dinner he could drive her into town in his new **Fiat**. In Latin *fiat* is a complete sentence: *Let it be done* (or *made*). In English *fiat* is a word that means a decree, an order coming from high places that *must* be carried out. Dictators rule by fiat; there are none to gainsay them (*gainsay*=against+say). But the automobile of that name is related to neither of these. It is made up of the first letters of *F*abbrica *I*taliana *A*uto-mobili *T*urino (the Italian automobile factory in Turin, a large industrial city in northern Italy where the cars are *fabric*ated).

In town, he might take her to a **milliner** (Milan, Italy) and buy her a stunning hat. A milliner was so called in England because as early as the sixteenth century he imported and sold fancy articles of apparel such as hats, ribbons, and gloves, originally manufactured in Milan. Or they might go to a department store where she would have a large assortment of cloths and *fabrics* to choose from:

CALICO: originally called Calicut cloth after the important sixteenth-century Indian seaport Calicut (not to be confused with Calcutta, a large inland city which has less pleasant historical associations).

CASHMERE: from Kashmir in the Western Himalayas, where goats produce this fine, soft wool.

DAMASK: from Damascus, capital of Syria, one of the most famous ancient cities of the world, where this fabric was first made.

DENIM: from Nîmes, a manufacturing town of Southern France. Its product was called *serge de Nîmes*, hence *denim.*

GAUZE: from Gaza, situated in the well-known Gaza strip.

LISLE: from Lille, France.

MADRAS: from Madras, India; a fine cotton cloth used in men's shirts and ladies' dresses.

TULLE: from Tulle, France; a thin, fine net.

TWEED: a famous river in Scotland.

WORSTED: from Worsted, England, famous for its weaving in the fourteenth century.

He could put everything she bought in a **duffel** bag (from Duffel, a Belgian town near Antwerp, where the coarse woolen cloth was first made).

After their wedding, when each had given the laconic answer, "I do," our young couple could live happily thereafter in a **bungalow**, a style of house first built in Bengal, India.

As you have probably guessed, the word **laconic** means short, brief, terse, concise, pithy, succinct. Any word with so many synonyms must be worth saying something about.

Sparta, one of the famous cities of ancient Greece, was located in a district called Laconia. The Spartans, as you remember, were a military community, and military men have always been famous for their economy in the use of words—in short, for being laconic. When Xerxes summoned the Spartan general Leonidas to surrender his arms, Leonidas answered, "Come and get them." Dispatches from the Spartan war front were just as terse. One great victory was announced as, "Persia is humbled"; another, bringing to an end the long and bloody Peloponnesian War, merely said, "Athens is taken."

In World War II one of our naval officers achieved

near perfection with this message: "Sighted sub; sank same."

But even authors can sometimes be laconic. Victor Hugo, shortly after *Les Miserables* appeared in the bookshops, wrote a letter to his publisher containing only the following:

?

to which the reply was:

!

Hugo was greatly pleased, for he was thus reassured that *Les Miserables* was selling wonderfully well.

3

FLOWERY LANGUAGE

The poetic language flowers often speak is understood easily when we think of a *forget-me-not*, a *morning glory*, or a *buttercup*. But sometimes an interpreter or guide is needed for even the most familiar and common of our flowers.

The **dandelion**, for instance, which James Russell Lowell addressed as

> Dear common flower, that grow'st beside the way
> Fringing the dusty road with harmless gold,

really has something to do with a lion. *Dandelion*, the English form of *dent de lion* (French for lion's tooth), is so called because the leaves have jagged tooth-like edges.

To its sword-shaped leaves we owe the name of **gladiolus**, which in Latin means a small sword (*gladius*, sword). A *glad*iator was one who fought to the death with a sword or some other weapon for the entertainment of the Roman public.

The much-prized flower **chrysanthemum** (shortened to mum), which is worn by young ladies at football games, is the "golden flower" (Greek *chrysos*, gold, plus *anthos*, flower). You probably know what an *anth*ology is but you may not know that the Greek poet Meleager compiled the first collection of Greek poems and named it an anthology (literally, a collection of flowers). For to him poems *were* flowers— flowers created by the minds of men and women. He tells us, therefore, that in his garland of flowers he wove in of one poet some lilies, of another many irises, and of Sappho, the greatest of Greek women poets, only "a few—but roses!"

The poet Longfellow once called all flowers "Stars that in the firmament do shine." But we call only one particular flower a star. In Greek, the word for star is *aster*.

A number of other flowers are named for real or fancied resemblances. This is easy to recognize in *Queen-Anne's lace, Indian pipe, jack-in-the-pulpit,* and *black-eyed Susan.*

But we need an interpreter again for **daisy**, which is really day's eye, the yellow center resembling the eye of the day, the sun. We don't need an interpreter for sunflower, with its large golden center.

The **hydrangea** is so called because of the cuplike shape of its seed capsule (Latin root *hydro*; Greek *hydor*, water). If you look hard enough at *hydor*, you can see it change to *water*. It flows clearly in *hydr*ant, *hydr*ophobia, *hydr*aulic, and *hydro*foil, a speedboat that skims the water with only some sheets of metal touching the surface. *Foil* means leaf or sheet, as in aluminum foil. It comes to us via French from the

Latin *folium*, leaf, from which we also get the words *foliage* and *defoliate*, to strip leaves off (*de*).

It was a Roman with a sense of humor who named the **nasturtium**. Because of its pungent odor, the flower was called a nose twister (Latin *nasus*, nose; plus *torquere*, *tortum*, twist, twisted). The root *tort* helps us to understand the real meaning of words like *tort*ure, dis*tort*, and con*tort*ionist. Even *torch* is related, for originally it referred to a twisted piece of cloth that served as a wick that would burn slowly.

Sometimes it is the color that produces the name. The **carnation** was originally flesh color. The Latin root *carn* means flesh. From it we get such fleshy words as in*carn*ate, in the flesh or as we say "in person"; and *carn*ivorous (flesh or meat eating; *vor* as in our words *devour, vor*acious, greedy in eating, and omni*vor*ous, eating all, *omni*, things).

The name **iris** acknowledges the many beautiful colors in which this flower appears, for Iris was the Greek goddess of the rainbow. From *iridis*, another form of *iris*, we get *irid*escent and *irid*escence, words that call attention to the shimmering rainbow colors. (Notice why there is only one *r* in these words.)

From mythology, too, comes the name of another flower—the **narcissus**. Narcissus was a handsome young man loved by a girl named Echo, but he gave her little attention. He saved his love for himself. One day, while leaning over a brook, he caught sight of his own reflection in the water. His self-admiration rooted him to the spot—and there he pined away and died. The gods taking pity on him changed him into a flower. Today many a narcissus grows near a brook bending towards it on its long stem when the breezes blow. The gods, in their equal justice, took pity on Echo, too. Her voice can still be heard among mountains and valleys mourning her lost love. The word *narcissistic* describes someone who is completely lost in admiration of himself.

It is hard to believe that such beautiful-sounding names of flowers as **begonia, camellia, dahlia, forsythia, fuchsia,** (pronounced few-sha), **gardenia, magnolia, poinsettia, wisteria** (sometimes written as wistaria), and **zinnia** are merely the last names of

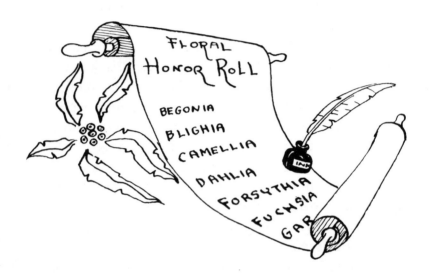

men—with the ending *ia* added. To prove it, here is an international botanic Who's Who, a floral honor roll:

BEGONIA: Michel Bégon, a seventeenth-century French naval officer, patron of botany, and governor of Santa Domingo.

CAMELLIA: George Josef Kamel (Latinized into Camellus), a seventeenth-century Moravian Jesuit, who is said to have introduced the camellia from the Far East.

DAHLIA: Professor Anders Dahl, an eighteenth-century Swedish botanist and pupil of Linnaeus, the eighteenth-century Swedish naturalist who established the system that classifies all plants by Latin names of genus and species.

FORSYTHIA: William Forsyth, nineteenth-century British botanist, who brought the shrub from China.

FUCHSIA: Dr. Leonhard Fuchs, a sixteenth-century German physician, professor of medicine, and botanist.

GARDENIA: Dr. Alexander Garden, an eighteenth-century Scottish botanist and zoologist who practiced for several years in South Carolina.

MAGNOLIA: Dr. Pierre Magnol, a seventeenth-century professor of medicine and director of the botanic garden at the French University of Montpelier.

POINSETTIA: Joel R. Poinsett, first United States Minister to Mexico in the early nineteenth century, who discovered the flower and brought it to the United States.

WISTERIA, WISTARIA: Dr. Caspar Wistar (1761–1818), physician and author of the first American book on anatomy. Through usage the flower is more often called *wisteria* than *wistaria.*

ZINNIA: Johann Gottfried Zinn, eighteenth-century professor of medicine at the University of Göttingen.

Who would be the most unlikely person to have a plant named after him? You may not believe it but it's Captain William Bligh—later Admiral—the notorious commander of "The Bounty," whose sailors mutinied against him in 1789 because of his ill-treatment of them and set him adrift in a lifeboat in the South Seas. The plant whose fruit he brought back from the East was called **blighia** (blye-ghee-a).

. 4 .

STORIES IN WORDS

Between the years 1577 and 1580, Francis Drake, making many stops, circumnavigated the globe. Since he was the first Englishman to do so, he was knighted in a private ceremony by Queen Elizabeth I.

Almost 400 years later, history repeated itself when another Elizabeth, Queen Elizabeth II, using Sir Francis Drake's sword, lightly tapped another Francis, Francis Chichester, on both shoulders for a similar achievement. This time TV cameras carried the ceremony, known as the **accolade**, to millions of English viewers.

Francis Chichester had returned from a 28,500 mile trip around the world. He had made that journey in 120 days all alone in a small sailboat. The ceremony took place at the very spot where Sir Walter Raleigh once laid down his cloak so that good Queen Bess might not soil her royal slippers.

The word **accolade** has a story of its own to tell. It comes from the Latin verb *accolare*, to embrace, *ac* (for *ad*), to, plus *collum*, neck. (That's why something worn around the neck is called a collar.)

Gregory of Tours, one of the early kings of France, performed the ceremony literally. He put his arms around the knight-to-be and kissed him on the cheek. The France of today carries on the tradition. When any military honor is conferred, the man so honored is kissed on both cheeks.

William the Conqueror, however, made use of his fist—gently, we suppose—when he knighted his son Henry. In more modern times a light tap with the flat blade of a sword on both shoulders has become the official way of conferring knighthood: the ceremony of the **accolade**.

Today *accolade* is in general use and much in vogue for any enthusiastic expression of praise. Thus a word that once meant only a special ceremony is today used to mean the highest praise, a great honor, or a great award.

Just the opposite might have happened to an illustrious citizen of ancient Greece when Athenian democracy—not knighthood—was in flower. So jealous were the Athenians of their democracy that when any citizen seemed on the way to becoming too powerful a vote would be taken. It was a strange kind of vote, because it was taken to decide whether, for the safety of the state, it might not be better to send such a citizen into exile for a period of years. The voting took place in the Agora, or market place. One type of ballot used was an oyster shell (Greek *ostrakon*) on which the name of the man to be **ostracized** was written. There had to be at least 6,000 votes to send a citizen into exile. He could return after five or ten years and have his property and social status restored to him. It was not considered a punishment, just a safeguard against possible dictatorial ambitions. Nevertheless, it wasn't fun. Nor is it fun to be ostracized today. For to be ostracized is to be socially excluded, to be cut off from those with whom you had once associated.

One little aside here. The voters in Athens cast their oyster shells, tiles, or shards (pieces of pottery) into a receptacle. Have you sometimes wondered why we say "cast a vote"? Here may be the answer.

Two thousand years later in a small village in County Mayo, Eire, an even stronger word than ostracize was invented. The rent collector of the district was a harsh man, ruthless in his methods. In 1880, local crops were bad, wages low, and rents high, and the townspeople appealed to the captain for help. He flatly refused their appeals.

Desperate, the villagers sought the advice of Father John O'Malley, the parish priest, and the aid of the Irish Land League. Among them, it was decided that the only way to meet the situation was for the townspeople to combine against the rent collector, no longer to have any dealings with him, to ostracize him. Laborers would refuse to work for him; tradesmen would refuse to serve him.

To insure solidarity, they needed an easier and stronger word than ostracism or social excommunication. It was Father O'Malley who gave them the word around which they could rally. "The Captain's name is Charles Cunningham Boycott," he said. "Very well, let us use his name. 'Tis a strong word. Let's **Boycott** him!" The villagers took up the cry and suited their actions to the word. Soon it was Captain Boycott who was desperate.

London papers picked up the word. Thereafter newspapers on the Continent began to flash it in their headlines. The countries of Europe incorporated it into their languages. In France, *to boycott* became the word *boycotter*; in Germany, *boycottiren*; in Italy, *boicottare*; and in Russia, *boycottirovat*. Over most of the world today, the word signifies one of the strongest actions an outraged community can take.

In the eighteenth century, British sailors serving under Admiral Edward Vernon found another way of expressing their resentment. To begin with, they nicknamed him "Old Grog," because he used to wear a large grogram (a cloth of coarse grain or texture, from French *gros grain*) coat flung loosely over his shoulders whenever the weather or his mood was nasty. In those days, sailors in the British navy were accustomed to getting a daily ration of rum. Therefore, in 1740, when Admiral Vernon issued an order to dilute the rum, his sailors contemptuously gave the name of **grog** to his mixture of rum and water. Today "Old Grog's" naval victories and adventures at sea are forgotten. He is remembered only for the water he put in his sailors' liquor.

In this roundabout way we got the word *grog* to mean any kind of liquor, and the adjective *groggy* to

describe a person who is dizzy or unsteady on his legs. When a prize fighter is groggy, he is punch drunk.

In a world like ours where emergencies frequently arise, the word **curfew** is often encountered. It means that between certain designated hours residents must stay indoors. They must keep off the streets. A curfew may be applied to the people of an entire city when it is occupied by enemy troops or only to those who live in areas where disturbances and riots have occurred.

In medieval Europe a curfew bell was rung every evening. At a time when almost all houses were built of wood and had no chimneys, fire was one of the great hazards of community living. As a safety measure, a warning bell was tolled at about eight or nine in the evening, ordering all townsmen to cover or extinguish their fires. French *couvre*, cover, plus *feu*, fire, became our word *curfew*. As long as danger from fire existed, the practice remained. The Pilgrims and Puritans brought the custom over with them to New England.

Another word connected with fire is concerned only with the smoke produced. Since 1274, upon the death of a pope, it has been the custom for the cardinals to choose a new pope at a meeting called a **conclave**, in rooms which are locked with (*con*) a key (*clavis*). The doors of the rooms are not opened again until they have come to a decision. They then fill the fireplace with a special kind of paper which gives off white smoke, signaling to the throngs in St. Peter's Square and to the world that a new pope has been chosen.

The word *conclave* is also used today in a more general sense for any secret or solemn meeting from which important decisions are expected. Other words we get from the root *clav*, key, are *clavichord* (*chorda*, string), a forerunner of the modern piano, and *clavicle*, the collarbone. Then there's the word *enclave* (*en*, in), used to describe the white ghettos of the past and the black ghettos of the present. In general, an enclave is a populated area *locked in* from the rest of the city or country. Vatican City is an enclave, a separate state within the city of Rome. So is Washington, D.C., since it isn't a part of any of the states that surround it.

In Washington, at a meeting of Congress in 1850, a debate on the Missouri Compromise was in progress. Felix Walker, representative from Buncombe County,

North Carolina, rose to speak. He went on and on pointlessly, boring his listeners. Despite the cries of impatience all around him, he continued. Finally, observing the disturbance, he stopped to tell his colleagues that he wasn't talking for them but for his constituents. The folks back home, he told them, expected him to speak for Buncombe. Thereafter, Buncombe became **bunkum** and finally the common slang or colloquial word **bunk.** When you hear someone say, "That's the bunk," he is implying that the other person is talking nonsense. To *debunk* is to clear away the nonsense or false or exaggerated opinions or claims and reveal the real facts.

. 5 .

WHAT'S IN A NAME?

Jersey School Suspends Youth for His Sideburns

Special to The New York Times
EDISON, N.J., May 24—After a
hearing that lasted 10 hours the Board
of Education of Edison Township suspended a 17-year-old honor student
from the Edison High School today for
having sideburns that they considered
too long.

I wonder whether any members of the Edison Board
of Education had ever heard of Ambrose Everett Burnside, a Union general, whose fame today is linked to
the sidewhiskers he wore rather than to any achievements on the battlefield. His long sidewhiskers were
first given the name of burnsides in his honor and then
later, to bring the word closer to its meaning, the
syllables were reversed and the more familiar word
sideburns came to be used.

By the way, General Burnside was once suspended
too—not because his sidewhiskers were too long, but
because he suffered a crushing defeat at the Battle of
Fredericksburg (Dec. 13, 1863). It is only fair to add
that later in civilian life he served as a member of Con-

gress from Rhode Island and became the governor of that state.

A general who was more effective as a military man was a seventeenth century Frenchman named Jean Martinet, who whipped an army into shape for Louis XIV by introducing a new system of military drill. He was obviously a severe taskmaster, for today the word **martinet** is applied to any strict disciplinarian (including a teacher!) who is rigid in manner and demands.

Another army man, a foot-soldier named Nicholas Chauvin, also contributed a word to our language. Though he was wounded seventeen times while serving in Napoleon's army, he would talk of nothing but the glory of fighting for Napoleon and the greatness of the Empire. His comrades, fed up with his constant chatter, ridiculed him for his super-heated patriotism and a new word was born—**chauvinism** (pronounced show-vin-izm). At first, the word characterized any exaggerated

expression of patriotism or nationalism. Today the word is not so restricted. It is used when someone shows a very strong attachment to any group. A male chauvinist, for example, is one who feels that only men have ever contributed anything of great importance to the progress of the world. Such a person is about as reasonable as the original Nicholas Chauvin.

Still another soldier, this time an American patriot, the then President of the United States, was willing to lend his name to a toy. In 1902 President Theodore Roosevelt went to Mississippi to settle a border dispute between Mississippi and Louisiana. For relaxation the popular "Teddy" Roosevelt took time out for hunting. One day a tiny bear cub wandered into the President's camp. Roosevelt, a big game hunter, refused to harm the little round ball of fur.

The *Washington Star* made the incident famous when it printed Clifford Berryman's cartoon of the event, showing President Roosevelt resting his gun and holding up his left hand in a gesture of forbearance. The caption under the cartoon, a pun of course, was "Drawing the line in Mississippi."

An enterprising toy manufacturer, seeing the cartoon, created a little stuffed bear and put it in the window of his store. Before the day was over, someone had bought it. Others like the first one were made and one was sent to the President. At the same time, he was asked for permission to name the bear after him and call it the **Teddy** Bear. In this way, according to the Ideal Toy Corporation of New York, the **teddy** bear got its name—and fame.

On the other hand, if you are the lone-wolf type, unattached, not bound by the expected loyalties, you may be called a "maverick." Samuel A. Maverick was a Texas cattle owner, who didn't bother to brand his calves. At first the word **maverick** was used only for unbranded cattle. Today it is used for those—usually politicians or statesmen—whose actions run counter to their party policy. They do not conform. They cannot be labeled. They act unpredictably. They are mavericks.

If someone does something that isn't too bright, he's likely to be called a "dunce"—a word that comes to us, paradoxically, from the name of a man who in his own time was famous for his great learning! For John Duns Scotus (the Scotsman) was no dunce. Far from it. He was a highly respected theologian of the thirteenth century.

In the sixteenth century, however, followers of his doctrines, called Dunsmen, violently opposed the teachings of the Renaissance. They were accused of being too stupid to understand the new learning. Name-calling followed, and the name they were called in derision was "Dunses." And so the name of a wise man has in its modern spelling, **dunce**, given us a word that has an exactly opposite meaning.

Another word with an uncomplimentary meaning is the word **tawdry**. It goes back to the time when fairs were held annually in Ely, England, in honor of St. Audrey. Among the most popular articles sold at the booths were cheap laces used as neckpieces. At first they were called St. Audrey laces. Then, as often happens in England when names are spoken with the

hurried British accent, St. Audrey became *tawdry*. Try
it.* Today *tawdry* is applied to any finery that is cheap-
ly showy, gaudy, or pretentious—anything in bad
taste.

Many other men's and women's names have given
us words, whose connection with the person has now
been forgotten. Here are some of the more interesting
"footprints in the sands of time" that they have left
behind them.

BLOOMERS: Mrs. Amelia Bloomer, a fighter for
women's rights, wore trousers on the lecture platform
and urged other women to do so as well. Today girls
wear bloomers in school gymnasiums.

BRAILLE: In 1829, Louis Braille, a Frenchman,
invented the system of raised dots that makes it possible for the blind to read.

CARDIGAN: We get the popular coat sweater from
the seventh Earl of Cardigan, who as commander of
the famous charge of the Light Brigade at Balaclava in
the Crimea, was the first Englishman to reach the
Russian lines.

DERRICK: This modern hoisting apparatus is
named for a famous hangman of the seventeenth
century who was in charge of a different kind of machine!

GUILLOTINE: This instrument that caused heads
to roll during the French Revolution was suggested by

---

*In the same way the French Saint Denis (pronounced san-de-nee)
gave us our name Sidney.

Dr. Joseph Ignace Guillotin, Paris physician and deputy to the National Assembly. It is not true that he invented the machine or that he perished by it.

GALVANIZE: Because of his experimentation with electricity and its effect on animals, Luigi Galvani of Bologna, Italy, has left us the words *galvanic* and *galvanize*. Besides its scientific meanings, the word *galvanize* has the meaning of to shock into action—as if by an electric current.

MESMERIZE: Franz Anton Mesmer believed there was a healing and magnetic power in his own hands, which he called "animal magnetism." In Vienna about 1775, he demonstrated his ability, not realizing that he was using suggestion and a form of hypnotism (from Greek *hypnos*, sleep). To mesmerize also means to cast a spell over.

PASTEURIZED: How safe we all feel knowing that the milk we drink and the butter and cheeses we eat are pasteurized. We owe this feeling of security to Louis Pasteur (1822–1895), a French chemist, who discovered the process. Today, all kinds of liquids are pasteurized, from apple juice to beer. It has become a magic word.

SANDWICH: We are able to put pasteurized butter on a slice of bread because of the fanatical addiction to gambling of the fourth Earl of Sandwich. One evening, unwilling to stop for dinner—what was happening at the gaming table was far more interesting—he ordered his "man" to bring him his roast beef wrapped in two protective slices of bread. And lo! a man's casual inventiveness made the quick lunch and the picnic a part of modern life.

SAXOPHONE: Antoine Joseph Sax was a nineteenth-century maker of musical instruments and inventor of this one.

SILHOUETTE: Etienne de Silhouette, finance minister of France (1759), levied drastic taxes on the aristocrats. In a spirit of revenge, it is said, they named the shadowed profile drawing or cutout after him in ridicule of his economies. Perhaps they felt he was taking away their substance and leaving only the shadow.

ZANY: This is both a noun and an adjective that movie critics like to apply to Jerry Lewis and to his clowning antics on the screen. The word comes from an Italian first name, Giovanni, the equivalent of our name John. Through a shortening to *gianni* and careless pronunciation the word became *zanni* (the Italian word for buffoon) and then in English *zany*.

It is fascinating to look at all the forms the popular name John takes in other languages and dialects: German—*Hans*, from *Johann*; French—*Jean*; Spanish—*Juan*; Scottish—*Ian*; Welsh—*Evan*; Russian—*Ivan*.

The word **spoonerism**, a slip of the tongue that interchanges the letters of two words in a phrase to get a humorous effect, deserves a section all to itself. The Rev. William A. Spooner (1844–1930) of New

College, Oxford, was celebrated for this habit of trans-
posing first letters. For example, in dismissing a student from the college—or sending him "down," as the
English say—he is supposed to have said, "You have
deliberately tasted two worms [wasted two terms] and
you can leave on the town drain [down train] to London."

It is reported that in conversation he referred to the
well-known, two-wheeled vehicle as "a well-*b*oiled
icicle" and to a friend's new cottage as "a *n*osy little
*c*ook." And it is said he would startle his parishioners
by saying, "One of the ushers will *s*ew you to your
*s*heets," or assuring them that something was as easy
to do as for "a camel to go through the *knee* of an
*i*dol."

. 6 .

ANIMALS HIDING OUT IN WORDS

Can you identify the animals hiding in the bold-type words in the following paragraph?

"**Philip** walked along Broadway wearing a **geranium** in his lapel and carrying an artist's **easel** under his arm. His exploits as an **aviator** seemed far away now as he **cynically** threaded his way through the heavy traffic. Suddenly a **taxicab** horn blew, startling him as if it were a **bugle**. There in the path of the **cab** stood a beautiful but **bewildered** young lady. **Muscles** taut, Philip **chivalrously** swept her on to the curb, thus narrowly averting a **tragedy**. Her grateful smile seemed to him an **auspicious** beginning of a beautiful friendship."

Traveling in disguise in this slightly "kooky" passage are two horses, one donkey, one dog, two goats, one deer, three birds, a bullock, and a mouse. Can you figure out who's who?

Philip is one of the horses, for the name is a combination of two Greek words: *philos* (loving) and *hippos* (horse), and that makes Philip a lover of horses. A *hippo*potamus is literally a river horse, and a *hippo*drome was in Greek times an oval track for horse and chariot races. You'll find "love" in each of the following *phil* words. So that you can figure out the meaning of each of them yourself, the meaning of the other part of the word is given to you:

phil*anthropy* (*anthropos*, "man" as in *anthrop*ology)
philo*soph*er (*sophos*, "wisdom")
phil*harmon*ic (*harmonia*, "harmony")
philo*logist* (*logos*, "word"; *ist*, "one who")
*Anglo*phile (*Anglo*, the English or things English)

The other horse is found in **chivalrous**. *Cheval* is the French word coming from *caballus*, the Latin word. Between the two, they account for such words as *chivalry*, *cavalcade* (now applied to any procession or parade), *cavalry*, and *cavalier*. In the Middle Ages the owner of a horse was a gentleman, a knight. These overtones cling to the word *chivalrous*.

Then, as now, the donkey was a beast of burden. In an artist's studio his burden is rather a pleasant one when he supports the artist's canvas. For an **easel** is a donkey, nothing more. The word comes from the Dutch *ezel* and is related to the more familiar German word *esel*, which like our donkey is also used as a term of abuse.

The first goat (Latin *caper*, goat) runs almost unseen through many of our words. If you cut *caper*s, you're behaving like a "kid," a young goat. If your mood changes suddenly—like a prancing goat—you are *capr*icious. A *capr*ice is a whim that can easily

change. A *cabr*iolet was a light, one-horse, two-seated
carriage that jounced along the cobblestone streets like
a goat. A **taxicab** is really a shortened form of taxi-
meter-cabriolet, which has been further shortened to
either taxi or **cab**.

The other goat is Greek. *Tragos* is a goat and *ode* is
a song so that the word tragedy really means a goat

song. Why? Nobody is certain why. One of the explanations is found in the ceremonies held in ancient Greece in connection with the worship of Dionysus (more commonly known as Bacchus) the god of wine. At the festival a goat was usually sacrificed to Dionysus. The choruses that were sung at the sacrificial rites were called goat songs, thus probably giving the name tragedy to the plays that later developed from these songs —such monumental tragedies as those written by Aeschylus, Sophocles, and Euripides, almost 2,500 years ago! (One extraordinary thing is certain: These playwrights are the only ones who are ever mentioned in the same breath with Shakespeare.)

When we call someone "Butch," we're going back to the word goat again, this time by way of the French. A butcher was so called because he slaughtered and sold the flesh of goats, (*bouc*, French for he-goat, becoming *boucher*, butcher).

The Latin word for bird is *avis*, so that an aviator is obviously someone who has learned to fly like a bird. Not so obviously, **auspicious** (*avi* + *spic*, Latin root meaning to look or observe) is also a bird word. In Roman times augurs were priests whose duty it was to take "auspices" on all state occasions, to observe birds in flight and determine from their cries, their number, and their direction whether the time was a favorable one for beginning some important undertaking. To in*augur*ate is, therefore, to begin with suitable and, it is hoped, *auspicious* ceremonies.

One of our best known birds has a dog's name and usually leads a dog's life. The *canary* (from *canis,* Latin for dog) gets its name from the Canary Islands, which in turn get their name from the large dogs the Romans found when they discovered the islands. A *canine* tooth is one pointed like a dog's.

A **cynic** (*kynos,* Greek for dog) is hardly a gay dog. We associate the word *cynical* with the less attractive canine qualities—the growling and snarling and backbiting. Diogenes has remained the most famous of the cynics, and his cynicism is classically illustrated by the story that he went around in broad daylight with a lighted lantern looking for an honest man.

But *cynosure,* which literally means a dog's tail, has a more pleasant connotation. One of the names the Greeks gave to the seven stars that we call the Little Dipper was Cynosura because of the resemblance of the constellation to the upturned curl of a dog's tail.

The North Star forms the outer end of the Little Dipper's handle. Sailors of old would scan the skies for Cynosura because it contained the bright star by which they could check their direction. It was their guiding star. John Milton made it stand for the center of attraction in another sense in the lines:

> Where perhaps some beauty lies,
> The cynosure of neighboring eyes.

Bugle was once an English word for a bullock or young ox (Latin *buculus*). *Bucolic*, a related word, refers to life in the country. A hunting horn was originally made of a "bugle's" horn with the tip cut off and was called a bugle horn. We've dropped the horn and left the animal.

Geranium comes to us from the Greek *geranus*, meaning a crane, the tall wading bird. The flower itself is often called a crane's bill because one of its parts is similar in shape to a crane's bill. *Pedigree* literally means a crane's foot (French *pied de grue*). If you've even seen the chart of a family tree you will notice the resemblance of the three lines showing descent to the footprints of a bird.

Muscle is from *musculus*, Latin for a small mouse. Rippling muscles look like a mouse running along under the skin. Even the Romans used the word in the same way. The shellfish called a *mussel* has the same origin.

Are you *bewildered*? If you are, it means that you are figuratively lost in the **wilderness**, and wilderness

literally means wild (*wild*), animal (*der*), and place
(*ness*). *Der* comes from the Anglo-Saxon *deor*, meaning animal. Today the word means one specific animal
—the deer—but in Shakespeare's time it still meant
all animals, for a character in *King Lear* talks about
"mice and rats and such small deer." The modern German *Tier* still means all the animals, and a Tiergarten
is a German zoo.

And now here are some more examples from our
own Who's Zoo of animal words:

AQUILINE is from *aquila*, Latin for eagle, and is
generally used to describe a nose that is shaped like an
eagle's beak.

ARCTIC comes from *arctos*, Greek for bear. The polar
meaning comes from the fact that the Greeks called the
two constellations near the North Pole the Great Bear
and the Little Bear—our Big and Little Dippers.

COWARD gets its meaning from the fact that a person so called retreats like a dog with his tail (French
coue, from Latin *cauda*) between his legs. For someone
who behaves in a cowardly fashion, we also have the
expression "to turn tail" and run away. In music, the
coda is the tailpiece, or concluding part, of a musical
composition.

DUPE, describing one who is easily deceived or
tricked, may go all the way back to a Latin word that
means pigeon and therefore parallels our use of the
word "pigeon" to characterize an "easy mark," a person easily deceived and taken advantage of.

TOADY is a shortening of the original word, *toad eater*, the name given to the boy who accompanied the "medicine man" at fairs held in England. At that time toads were considered poisonous, and the crowd would gasp when they saw the boy swallow, or pretend to swallow, a toad. As the boy grimaced in agony, his master would quickly reassure the crowd. Producing a bottle containing a harmless and worthless liquid, he would pour some of it into his "toady's" mouth. A miraculous cure, of course, was immediately effected, and the "medicine man" would sell many bottles of his potion. The word *toady*, therefore, describes a person who, like the boy at the fair, will do anything to please someone in a superior position—a cringing, fawning hanger-on.

TERRIER, from *terra*, Latin for earth, is a dog that pursues animals into their hideouts in the earth. From

terra we get the words *terr*ain, *terr*itory, *terr*arium, an aquarium with earth substituted for water (*aqua*), and the *terr*estrial globe, a fancy name for our planet Earth.

VACCINATE reminds us that we are partly indebted to the cow (Latin *vacca*) for our immunity against smallpox. In 1798, Edward Jenner, an English physician, perfected a serum made of cow pox (*variolae vaccinae*) to fight the dread disease.

The cow in **herds** (Latin root *greg*) gives us a number of useful words. A *greg*arious person likes the company of others. When people herd together (*con*) they con*greg*ate. If someone is set off (*se*) from the others, he is se*greg*ated. One who stands out (*e*) from the herd is remarkable, e*greg*ious; but that word today is used only in a bad sense, as in an egregious blunder, an egregious fool, something or someone remarkably bad. Ag*greg*ate means the total, and that means, "That's all!"

. 7 .

SLANGUAGE

Most slang, like the word *kookie*, used in the preceding chapter, is a short quick thrust—here today and gone tomorrow. Some of it becomes feverishly popular for a while. "So's your Aunt Tilly," "Your father's mustache," and "23 skiddoo" had their brief run. They are now merely amusing museum pieces, tags to identify a past age. The best slang, however, lasts a long time because it has roots in the imagination and because it often takes a vivid short cut to our thoughts.

Such slang is soon promoted to what we call colloquial, or conversational, status and sometimes is even accepted in the best society. Our statesmen and diplomats would find it hard to get along without such colorful expressions as "left holding the bag," "getting out on a limb," "pulling the rug out from under," "rolling out the red carpet," "slinging mud at," etc. Such expressions will last as long as the picture remains true and the color remains vivid.

Believe it or not, there are slang or colloquial expressions that have lasted thousands of years. The Greeks and Romans had words for them. Today we use words derived from the Latin and Greek without realizing that if we were to look into their literal mean-

ings we would find many colorful modern expressions.

For instance, "to put something over on" or the more modern "put-on" is the literal meaning of **impose** (*poser*, Latin for "to put or place" plus *im*, "on or in"). The word **impostor** describes one who (*or*) tries "to put something over on" others. From the root *pos*, we get *com*pose (put together), *inter*pose (place *between*), *de*pose (put someone *down* from his *posi-*tion), *de*position (a statement you put *down* in writing), and *op*pose (to place yourself *against*).

If you are one of those people who are always "on the dot," you are **punctual** (*punctus*, Latin for point). Punctuation is merely the placing of points—dots, commas, semicolons, etc.—in the right places.

If you get your **share**, you are getting your "cut." For *share* comes from an Anglo-Saxon word that means to cut. That's what *shears* do. And a *shard* or *sherd* is a shortening of the word *potsherd* (pronounced pot-shirred), all of which mean a broken piece of pottery.

If you are "broke," you are **bankrupt** (*rupt*, Latin root meaning broken). When you "butt in" or "bust in on" something, you are *inter*rupting. If you suddenly break off what you are saying, you are being *ab*rupt. If what you say or do, breaks up what others have agreed or planned on, you are a *dis*ruptive influence. A *cor*rupt act is one that breaks *with* accepted ethical or moral standards.

If you are "wise to things" or "wised up," you are **sophisticated**. The Greek root *soph* means wise. A *philo*sopher, for example, is one who *loves* (*phil*) wisdom. A sopho*more* is a wise fool! (*Moron* comes from a Greek word meaning foolish.)

If you "catch on" easily, you **comprehend** or **apprehend** things quickly, for *prehendere* is Latin for "to grasp or get hold of." An **apprentice** is one who is "learning the ropes," convenient things to hold on to.

If you "play ball with" or "play along with," you are really in **collusion** with someone. The Latin roots *lud* and *lus* mean play. A *pre*lude *pre*cedes a play. An *inter*lude is the time *between* acts of a play. "Tricks are being played on" your eyes when you see an *illusion*, a mirage, something that isn't really there.

You are going "around in circles" when you search for something, for **search** goes back ultimately through

French (*chercher*) to the Latin word *circus*, which means circle. Picadilly Circus in London is not a show under a huge tent but a center where many streets meet —like Columbus Circle in New York City. A *circus* is so called because it is usually held in a circular arena.

You are "sitting pretty," in a sense, when you **supersede** (note the spelling) someone. You are literally sitting (*sed*, Latin root meaning *sit*) over (*super*) someone else. Your *re*sidence is a place where you hope you can sit *back* and relax. When you sit close *to* your work, you are *as*siduous, diligent, industrious. If you are a *dis*sident, you are taking a position of opposition or a seat *against* the accepted opinion.

If you are *haughty* about it, you are "uppity," you are holding your "nose *high* in the air," and you may be told to "get off your *high* horse," for *haut* in French means high. You may even be called **supercilious**, a word that comes from Latin *super* (above) and *cilium* (eyelid). The *supercilium* was the eyebrow. The raising of the eyebrows has always been considered an expression of haughtiness.

If in speaking to someone you use "double talk," you are **equivocating** (Latin *equi*, equal, plus *voc*, voice). The predictions of the Greek oracles could often be interpreted in two ways—purposely so. Once when a great king asked the oracle at Delphi whether it was an auspicious time to engage the enemy in battle, the answer was, "On that day, you will destroy a great empire." He didn't realize until too late that the empire would be *his own*. The prediction was not wrong!

At the end of Shakespeare's play, Macbeth calls the three witches equivocators because they use words "in a double sense":

> They keep the word of promise to our ear,
> And break it to our hope.

If you should be "burned up" by equivocation or all "het up," you're really **incensed**, from a form of the Latin verb *incendere*, to burn, as in incendiary bomb, for instance. The *cens*er that is swung in religious rituals holds burning in*cense*.

You are literally "jumping on someone" when you **insult** him. *Sult* is a Latin root meaning jump or leap. When you are *ex*ultant (the *s* is swallowed up by the *x*) you are "jumping out of (*ex*) your skin" with joy. *De*sultory reading or activity is aimless, jumping from one thing to another, with no definite goal in mind.

If you **humiliate** someone, you are "treating him like dirt"; you are making him "feel low" (Latin word *humus*, earth, as well as the English word *humus* meaning a rich soil). To dig something up is to *exhume*.

When a person says, "I thought I'd die," he probably feels **mortified** (Latin root *mort*, death). Thus a *mort*al wound is a deadly one. In detective stories a *postmortem* examination is one made after (*post*) the murder. Discussions *after* the game is over of what should have been done are also called *postmortems*.

When you are **deterred** from an action, you are "scared off" (Latin *de*, off, plus *terrere*, to frighten), as in *terrify, terror, terrible, terrific*. However, when you are **circumspect**, you "look around" (Latin *circum* around, plus *spect*, look) before you do anything. You wait to see whether "the coast is clear"; you are cautious.

The "wool is being pulled over your eyes," when you allow yourself to be **inveigled** into doing something you really don't want to do. Inveigle comes from *aveugle*, the French word for blind, which ultimately goes back to *oculus*, the Latin word for eye.

If you get tangled up in the wool, if you are all "tied up in knots," you are **perplexed** (*per*, thoroughly, plus *plexus*, Latin for interwoven or knotted). The *solar plexus* is that spot in the abdomen where important nerves interlace.

But if you are able to "bounce back" easily from such situations you are **resilient** (*re*, Latin for back, plus *sil*, Latin root meaning leap or spring). You jump or spring back easily from setbacks.

When you **compile** a series of words like this you (or I, in this case) are really stealing (Latin root *pil*, as in *pil*lage or *pil*fer) and putting together (*com*) words from many sources. This is sometimes a necessary part of research. The question you might ask of a compiler is, "Did you raid any good books lately?"

Once when Charles Lamb was accused of plagiarizing (a polite word for appropriating someone else's ideas) he wrote: "I milked twenty cows to get the milk, but the butter I churned was my own."

. 8 .

SUPERSTITION AND PREJUDICE EMBEDDED IN WORDS

The night sky—with its millions of stars, its planets, and the moon with its ever-changing face—has always filled man with wonder and awe, and sometimes with fear. It is not surprising, therefore, that a number of superstitions have grown up around these heavenly bodies.

Words coming down to us from the moon and stars preserve for us a record of some of these superstitions. **Lunacy** and **lunatic**, for example, come from *luna*, the Latin word for moon. (French *lundi*, Italian *lunedi*, German *Montag* are all words for moonday, or Monday.) It was once believed that the changes of the moon influenced one's mental condition, might actually bring on a kind of insanity. You will find *moon-struck* in your dictionary with just such a meaning.

The word *bedlam*, which we associate with mad uproar, screaming, and confusion, is ultimately derived from the name of the town of Bethlehem. How? The London priory and hospital called St. Mary of Bethlehem, founded in 1247, was in 1402 set aside exclusively as a lunatic asylum for the violently insane. It is not difficult, therefore, to see how *bedlam*, a slurred

53

pronunciation of Bethlehem, came to have its present meaning.

Though there are few today who fear the power of the moon, there still are many who look upon the stars as beacon lights of their destinies. The word **disaster** shows us how deep-rooted this belief is. The Greek word for star is *aster*; the Latin word, *astrum*. One of the meanings of the prefix *dis* is *contrary to* or *against*. A *disaster*, therefore, is something contrary to the stars —contrary to the "lucky star" under which you were born.

Astrology, the art of predicting events from the location of the stars and planets, is one of the world's oldest professions. It flourishes in many parts of the world today and is probably most honored in some parts of northern India. Astrologers are consulted there, the way oracles once were in ancient Greece or Rome.

I heard of a young couple in India who would, by any standards, certainly be considered modern and sophisticated. She was a graduate of a university in the United States. He was an educated, well-traveled man of the world. Nevertheless, they went to see an astrologer to find out whether, before taking that important step in ther lives, it was an auspicious time to be married. "Not for three weeks yet," the astrologer solemnly advised them. "The stars and planets will not be in favorable conjunction for at least 20 days." And they took his advice!

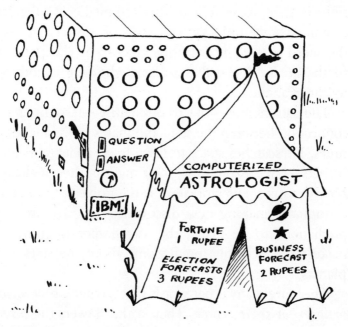

Newspapers have reported the predicament of an astrologer in India who incorrectly predicted an election result. Unperturbed by his failure, he explained that astrologers today really needed the help of computers to do their work accurately, and he complained that they are hard to come by in India!

But before any feeling of smugness sets in, let me remind you that the newspaper with the largest circulation in the United States has a column called "Your Stars Today," which daily advises, encourages, and warns its readers. If you send its astrologer 25 cents and the date of your birth, you will receive a horoscope for the entire year.

The word **dismal** (Latin *dies mali*, evil days) fits right in here, for it tells us that the medieval calendar contained some unlucky days, days of ill-omen. Today the word *dismal* means only gloomy or cheerless. A football team that makes a dismal showing is nothing to cheer about.

The astronomer—the true scientist—recognizes no connection between the stars and man's individual destinies. He searches space to learn more about stars and planets—their magnitude, their motion, their makeup, *their* destinies. His workshop is the universe, and he is continually making new discoveries. If there are any predictions to be made, the astronomer is going to make them, scientific predictions, about the stars and planets.

There are many other words that have the root *astro*, or *aster*, at their center. There's the flower, the *aster*, already mentioned and the little star, the *asterisk* (*), which directs you to a footnote at the bottom of the page. Our modern word *astronaut* is literally a sailor (Greek, *nautes*) among the stars. *Nautical*, of the sea, and *nausea*, literally seasickness, are related words. The many other *astro* combinations, like *asteroid*, *astral*, *astrolabe*, belong in the vocabulary of the astronomer.

PREJUDICE

City people have always felt superior to their country cousins; they have always looked down on those living in rural areas. How far back these prejudices go can be seen in some of the words used today. Consider such words as *boor*, *savage*, and *villain*. None of us would feel flattered to be called any of these. Yet once, before the corroding influence of prejudice began its work, they were perfectly respectable words.

Boor meant a farmer, nothing more. We see it in our word *neighbor*, which merely meant a *nigh* (near) *bor* (farmer). The German word for farmer is *Bauer*.

Savage comes via French from Latin *silva*, woods, and at first it meant one who lived in the forest. *Pennsylvania* was once William Penn's woods.

A **villain** was at first merely a servant working in a *villa*, Latin for a farmhouse. The word *village* is a community of farmhouses.

Webster's Third New International Dictionary gives the following synonyms for *boor*: *churl*, *lout*, *clown*, *bumpkin*, *clodhopper*, *hick*, *yokel*, *rube*, all implying rudeness or ignorance or clumsiness or any combination of them. Of these words **churl** and **clown** originally meant farmers, or peasants. For us, even the word

peasant has been so corroded that we reserve it for farmers of foreign countries. Nobody would think of calling an American or British farmer a peasant.

Hick, by the way, is not a modern word. It was used as early as the sixteenth or seventeenth century in England for a country bumpkin, a clumsy, ignorant fellow. But Hick, like Dick, was merely a nickname for Richard, and now appears only in last names such as Hickson and Hixon. Hob, like Bob, was a nickname for Robert, but it too is now used only in the last name Hobson. Rube is, of course, a nickname for Reuben.

Most "country" words seem to stand for everything that is uncouth, bad-mannered, or unsophisticated, but somehow "city" words usually describe the more attractive human traits. An **urbane** (pronounced ur-BAYN') person is polished in manner and style. Urbane comes from *urbs*, the Latin word for city, which also gives us the word *urban*, as in *urban renewal*. The surrounding areas of a city—its environs—were called *suburbs* (*sub*, under) reminding us that cities were once built on hills or heights and thus became natural fortresses.

Civil and **civilized** come from a Latin word from which we also get *civic* and the word *city* itself. **Courteous** and **courtly** come from the word *court* where courtiers met to pay homage to and serve their king and queen.

Vulgus is the Latin word for the multitude, the common people, giving us the word *divulge*, which means to make public, to tell people. But it also gives us words coated with prejudice such as **vulgar**, **vulgarity**, and·

mob, which is a shortened form of *mobile vulgus*, the easily *moved*, the changeable, the fickle crowd.

Finally, there is a group of words that are examples of both superstition and prejudice. A **dexterous** person, literally a right-handed one (Latin *dexter*, right), is a skillful or an *adroit* person. **Dexterity** means not only physical or mechanical skill but also mental quickness or *adroitness*. *À droit* is French for to the right, An *ambidextrous* person is one who literally has two right hands, since he can use either hand with equal efficiency.

On the other hand—the left—we uncover undesirable and unflattering connotations. A left-handed compliment refers to something said maliciously. What comes in from "way out in left field" has something unexpected about it.

Gauche, French for left, is a word used to mean clumsy, awkward, even socially inept. **Gawky**, a related word, emphasizes the clumsiness somewhat more. The Latin word for left is **sinister**! It is used now only in its suggestion of something malevolent and evil.

It is, of course, needless to add that there is no foundation for all this. Some of the brightest and most creative students I have ever taught were left-handed.

One of the world's greatest geniuses in science, as well as art, Leonardo da Vinci, was left-handed. So were Alexander the Great, who wept because there were no more worlds to conquer, and "Sandy" Koufax, one of the greatest baseball pitchers of all time. Finally, there are the Beatles, two of whom—Ringo Starr and Paul McCartney—are left-handed. Is further proof needed?

· 9 ·

TAKE A NUMBER FROM
ONE TO TEN

Our ancestors counted on their fingers. That is probably why in almost all parts of the world the decimal system is used. **Decimal** comes from the Latin word ten, *decem*; and **finger** probably comes from a word related to the German word for five, *fünf*.

Roman numbers show us rather clearly their origin in man's fingers. (*Digits*, another word for numbers from one to nine, comes from the Latin word *digitus*, meaning finger or toe.) The Roman numbers I, II, III, and IIII are obviously only a graphic representation of the number of fingers held up. V represents the four fingers separated from the thumb. Two V's one on top of the other thus, X, become X, or ten. Later on IV became four, the smaller number at the left being subtracted from the larger number on the right. In this way nine was written as IX rather than VIIII.

ONES

E pluribus unum, the motto of our country, means "out of many—one," for out of thirteen colonies, and ultimately fifty states, has been forged *one* mighty nation, one **union**. From *uni*, the Latin root that gives us *uni*on, we also get *uni*ty, *uni*fy (to make one), *uni*t, and *uni*form. *Uni*lateral actions are one-*sided*. A thing is

*uni*que when it is the only one of its kind.

When we sing in *uni*son, all of us try to sing one and the same sound. The Latin root *son*, "sound," yields such an interesting word as *person*, which meant originally a Greek actor's mask, containing a metal mouthpiece, through (*per*) which the *sound* came out somewhat amplified. The word later was applied to the character wearing the mask. When you read a play by Shakespeare, you will see on the page opposite the first act the heading *Dramatis Personae*, "the characters (or persons) of the play."

The Greeks, however, had another word that they used for one, which appears in English as *mono* and really means single. From it we get such words as *mono*cle (literally a single *eye*), *mono*poly (a single control), *mono*gram, (a single letter), *mono*tonous (a single, unchanging manner of speaking), and *mono*-

lith (a single *stone*, one of tremendous size like the famous ones at Stonehenge in England). We use the adjective *monolithic* to describe organizations, societies, or political parties that are as solid and unified as a huge slab of stone. A *monk* is so called because he lives *alone* in a *mon*astery.

For the word *first*, the Romans used *primus*. The *Prime* Minister, sometimes called the *Prem*ier (from French) is the first ranking minister. A *prem*iere is a first performance. When you *prime* a pump or carburetor, you are performing a necessary first operation to get it working. *Prim*ary, *prim*itive, *prim*er, all deal with first things. So does *prim*eval, which refers to the earliest age, the first period of time (*eval*). Thus the so-called Middle Ages are *medieval*, and things existing at the same time are *coeval*.

TWOS

Two is company, and just see the company we're in! *Duo*, *bi*, *bis*, *bini*, *ambi*, and *di* all have something to do with two. To be in *dou*bt or to be *du*bious about something is to be of *two* minds about it. Interestingly enough, the German word for doubt is *Zweifel*—with *Zwei*, the German word for two, sticking right out of it. *Duo*, besides being a word by itself, of course, gives us *du*et and *du*al.

"Bis," adopted by French and Italian, is a cry we sometimes hear at concerts or at the opera. Like "Encore!" it means "Again!" or "Once more," "Twice."

Bi gives us bi*cameral*, having two *chambers*—legis-
lative—like our Congress; bi*sect*, to *cut* into two, (there
is no such word as *disect*; it is *dissect*); bi*cycle*, two
wheels; bi*lingual*, using two languages; and bi*partisan*,
composed of members of two *parties*.

Bini gives us bin*oculars*, literally two *eyes*; to *com*-
bine, to put two and two together (*com*); and the in-
creasingly important word *binary*. Although it is used
in other sciences, today *binary* is most important in
mathematics. The binary system of numerical notation
is the basis for the lightning calculations made by computers. In a fraction of a second they can perform opera-
tions it might take a mathematician almost a whole day
to complete.

It is called binary because the system uses the number
two as a base and the only two numbers used are zero
and one. For there are only two possibilities electronic-
ally. When the current is on—one; when the current is
off—zero. Each digit, either a 1 or a 0, is called a **bit**,
a telescoping of the words *bi*nary and dig*it*.

In computer mathematics 1001 equals 9. How?
Working *from right to left*, the first number remains 0
or 1, the next one is multiplied by 2, then by 4, then
8, then 16, then 32, and so on. It can be seen that the
first 1 on the left in 1001 is in the 8 position; thus $8 +
1 = 9$. What does 11010 equal? Again reading from
right to left we get $0 + 2 + 0 + 8 + 16 = 26$.
It's as easy as that!

An *ambiguous* statement is one that may be understood in two or more ways. If you are *ambivalent* about anything, it means that you are *both* attracted and repelled at the same time.

When you are faced with a *dilemma*, it is different. You then are confronted with two choices, each equally unfavorable—or sometimes favorable but presenting a difficult choice. There is, for example, the fable of the donkey that was tied to a stake within reach of two bundles of hay at exactly equal distances from him to the right and to the left. He could not make up his mind in which direction to go. The dilemma was too great for him. He starved to death!

THREES

From the element *tri* (Latin), we get the obvious words *tri*cycle (three wheels), *tri*partite (involving three parties to an agreement), *tri*pod (a stand having three feet). *Tri*vial comes from *tri* and *via*, Latin for *road* or *way*. What one heard at the intersection of three roads was usually unimportant gossip, hence trivial. A *troika*—Russian, of course—is a carriage drawn by three horses abreast or just a team of three horses.

FOURS

The Romans used *quattuor* for *four* and *quartus* for fourth. From them we get *quartet*, *quadru*ped (having four feet), *quart* (one-fourth of a gallon), *quarter* (one-fourth of a dollar) and *quad*rangle. *Farthing*, related to our word four, was until 1961 a British coin, once worth one-fourth of a penny.

FIVES

Quintus is Latin for fifth and gives us *quint*uplets, *quint*essence (literally the fifth essence, the purest or highest; the first four *essenti*als, according to Greek philosophers are earth, air, fire, and water). In one of his melancholy moods, Hamlet, speaking of man, exclaims, "And yet, to me, what is this quintessence of dust?"

The Greek root for five is *penta,* giving us *Penta*teuch (the first five books of the Old Testament) and *pent*agon (a five-sided figure). When spelled with a capital letter it is the five-sided building that houses the United States Department of Defense.

SIXES

Sex and *hex* sound alike and are English words, but here they are just six of one (Latin *sex*) and a half-dozen of the other (Greek *hex*). *Sex*tet is obvious, but *siesta* is not. How, you may ask, does *siesta* (Spanish from *sexta hora*, Latin for sixth hour) come to mean a midday nap or rest? The hours of the day used to be counted from six in the morning; thus the sixth hour was twelve o'clock, the hottest part of the day. A *sex*tant is that very important navigators instrument whose arc is one-sixth of a circle. *Hex* gives us *hex*agon (a figure having six sides) and *hex*ameter (a line of verse having six metrical feet). For example:

Biting my truant pen, beating myself for spite,
"Fool," said my Muse to me, "look in thy heart and write."
Sir Philip Sidney (1554–1586)

SEVENS

Seven is one of the magic numbers. Shakespeare writes about the seven ages of man. At baseball games we stretch for luck during the seventh inning. In the Bible we are told of the seven years of plenty followed by seven years of famine. A *sept*uagenarian is one who has lived his Biblically allotted three score years and ten. And then there's September. Anyone who can count knows, however, that September is not the seventh month. But it used to be. Before 45 B.C., the old Roman year began in March and was followed by April, May, June, Quintilis, Sextilis, September, October, November, December, January, and February. When Julius Caesar reformed the calendar in 45 B.C., he made January the first month, thus making September the ninth month.

Well, what happened to Quintilis and Sextilis? History gives us the answer. After the death of Julius Caesar, Quintilis was changed to Julius in his honor and has come down to us as July. In the same way, the month Sextilis was changed to Augustus to honor the victories of Augustus Caesar in 8 B.C., and so our month August. And a good thing, too! Can you imagine a prosecutor in one of those TV courtroom scenes wagging an accusing finger at a witness and shouting,

"Where were you on the night of Sextilis the six-teenth?"

EIGHTS

The Latin root in words meaning *eight* is *oct*, giving us *oct*agonal (eight-sided), *octo*pus (eight feet), *oct*ave (a stretch of eight notes), *Octo*ber, and *octo*genarian (someone in his eighties).

NINES

We talk about "a nine days' wonder," "a cat with nine lives," possession being "nine points of the law," but we get only a few words from the Latin words *novem* for nine and *nonus* for ninth. There are *Novem*-ber, *nov*ena (a nine-day period of prayer), and *noon*, which comes from *Nona hora*, the ninth hour. This used to designate a three-o'clock church service (nine hours after six o'clock). When the time of the church service was changed to midday, the meaning of *nona* changed, too. And so *noon* means midday.

TENS

December comes from *decem*, Latin for ten, as do *decim*al and *dime*. And also *dean*! In Roman times, *decanus* meant a leader of ten soldiers. Later, the title *dean* was applied to an officer in a cathedral or an in-stitution of learning such as a college or a high school, where it has completely lost its limited significance of ten.

When our newspapers tell us that an army has been *decim*ated, they mean it has been practically destroyed.

The earlier meaning of decimated, however, was to kill one in ten as a punishment for mutiny. *Annihilate* would be a better word for total destruction because it means to reduce to nothing, Latin, *nihil*. And that's a number, too—zero—a most important number in our electronic age of computers.

. 10 .

WORDS THAT MEAN MONEY

It was Christmas eve of the year 1939, and the snow lay knee-deep on the campus of the Spanish-American Normal School at El Rito, New Mexico. The headmaster was already in bed when a little past midnight he was awakened by the ringing of the doorbell. There in the snow stood a farmer and his two little children, behind them a flock of sheep, above them a waning moon and a sky full of stars. The farmer had brought the children to the school for a year's stay; the twenty-six sheep were in payment of the fee; the moon and stars were silent witnesses.

Without knowing it the farmer was reenacting history, ancient history. He was going back to a time before money existed, when a man's wealth was reckoned by the number of cows, sheep, and pigs he possessed, and the chief medium of exchange was cattle. By using sheep to pay for his children's tuition and board, the farmer was dramatizing the history of several of our words associated with money.

Fee, for instance comes from the word *feoh*, which among the Anglo-Saxons meant any cattle. (The modern German word *Vieh*, pronounced fee, means only

that.) *Pecus*, the Latin word for cattle, gives us the word **pecuniary**, relating to money, and **impecunious**, which means habitually *without* money. Yes, and our word **peculiar**, too. For example, what might be given by a father to his son becomes the son's own possession, *peculiar* to him. Since what is one's own is personal and may seem odd or queer to others, *peculiar* has come to mean strange.

Peculiarly enough, our word money, through an accident of history, is related to such words as ad*mon*ish (from Latin *monere*, to advise or warn), *mon*itor, pre*mon*ition. In 390 B.C., the Gauls under their leader Brennus made one of their most successful attempts to conquer Rome. Late one night the soldiers of Brennus were getting ready to storm one of the strategic hills of the city. According to legend—not history—the sacred geese in the Temple of Juno heard the noise of the preparations and cackled a warning. The aroused defenders quickly manned their posts and saved Rome from destruction, though not from a long siege and the subsequent payment of ransom.

To honor the goddess, her temple from that time on —so the story goes—was called the Temple of Juno *Mon*eta (Juno the Warner). Years later, when the Romans chose this very temple to mint their first coins, they helped to coin our words *mon*ey, *mon*etary, and *mint*.

But money is a late development in the story of civilization. At one time or another in man's existence (and even today in some places), shells, tobacco, furs, rice, tea, and ivory served as money. In colonial Virginia, tobacco was recognized officially as money. One historian tells us that a clergyman's salary was about 16,-000 pounds of tobacco a year and a schoolteacher's about 8,000.

From the Latin word for salt (*sal*), we get the word **salary**, which shows us how all-important this commodity was in the days before refrigeration. The Latin *salarium* was "money allowed each soldier for the purchase of salt." Our familiar expression "to be worth one's salt" recognizes this association.

A gold piece that was coined in the time of the Caesars was called a *solidus* (solid) *nummus* (coin), or "hard cash." A member of the army, who served for money, thus became a **soldier**. Through French we get the English word **solder**, an alloy which when melted makes two metals solid. A *numismatist,* as you know, is one who collects coins.

But even when metals became the medium of exchange they were not minted into coins. The 1,000 pounds of gold that the Romans had to pay as ransom to Brennus in 390 B.C. were weighed on scales. The story is told that while the Romans were piling their precious metal high, the arrogant leader of the Gauls hurled his sword on the opposite side of the scales, crying *"Vae Victis!"* (Woe to the conquered!) and thus increased the amount of their ransom.

The names of several coins show this connection with weight. The Biblical *shekel* was originally a unit of weight. In more modern times we have the English pound. The Latin for pound is *libra*, giving us the pound sign (£), and the abbreviation *lb*. Italy and Turkey use the *lira* which also comes from *libra*. Most of the South American countries use the *peso*, from Latin *pensum*, weight.

Ex*pense* literally means weighed *out* (ex). Com*pens*ation is a balancing of work with (*com*) payment. When you are *pensive* you are weighing things in your mind. Look up the words *ponder* and *deliberate* in a dictionary and you will see that they, too, are concerned with weight. It has never been easy to think!

Through another accident of minting, our dollar is associated with dales and valleys. In 1518, coins were minted from the silver found in the mines in Joachimstal, a valley in Bohemia. The large coin produced there was first known as a *Joachimstaler* and later as a

taler (*thal*, German for *dale* or valley). The Dutch word was *daler* and finally we have the American **dollar**, which was officially adopted as the money unit of the United States by the resolution of Congress passed on July 6, 1785.

Most of us regard as slang the purely American word **buck**. However, according to John Bakeless, biographer of Daniel Boone, *buck* is really a return to a word our pioneers and trappers used. The deerskins they traded brought from forty cents to four or five dollars each. These skins were classified as "bucks" or "does." The larger and more valuable skins that brought in the dollars to the traders were called "bucks."

Cent is a Latin element meaning one hundred or a hundredth. Witness such words as *cent*ury, *cent*ennial, *cent*ipede (an insect with many, many feet) and per*cent*.

A *mill*, no longer existing as an American coin, comes from a Latin word meaning a thousand. A *mile* (Latin *mille passus*) was originally a thousand paces —not quite a mile unless you take giant steps.

Several other words associated with money have interesting backgrounds. Here are some:

ASSETS comes from *assez*, the French word for enough. In other words assets are things on the plus side.

DEFICIT, on the other hand, is entered in red. It is a complete one-word Latin sentence meaning "It is lacking." Nothing could be clearer.

FISCAL, having to do with financial matters, comes from *fiscus*, a Latin word meaning a basket made of twigs used as a purse. A later word *fiscalis* meant "relating to the public treasury." To *confiscate*, therefore, means to seize for the public treasury or by official authority.

Government budgets and expenses are figured for a fiscal year, not a calendar year. In the United States the fiscal year ends on June 30; in Great Britain and Canada on March 31.

PICAYUNE means small or insignificant because a picayune was a small coin, worth about six cents, once widely used in New Orleans.

TALENT today means a natural endowment or ability because of the parable told by St. Matthew (XXV, 14–30). Originally a talent was a unit of money worth 3,000 shekels.

Have you cut any coupons lately? Then you are doing exactly what the word tells you to, for *coup*on comes from *coup*er, the French word "to cut," (and the preferred pronunciation is KOO-pon!).

. 11 .

IT'S ALL GREEK TO ME

When someone wants to let you know that he's reading something *in English* that he doesn't understand, he is likely to say, "It's all Greek to me."

On an unusual TV program, Melina Mercouri, the vivacious Greek actress, served as guide for a tour of her country. She began her program by addressing her TV audience directly:

"You do not speak Greek? No? Yes!

"When you **telephone** to your **physician**, you are speaking Greek.

"When you tell him your **symptoms** and he is **sympathetic**, you are speaking Greek.

"You are watching me now on **television**. Greek.

"And it is all done with **electricity**; and that is Greek, too.

"You do not speak Greek? No? I say, Yes!"

What she was really saying was that English words have so many Greek words embedded in them that you know more Greek than you realize. To which I want to add that if you know what some of these Greek roots mean, you will know your own language better.

Let us take Melina Mercouri's first "Greek" word *telephone* and develop our own switchboard. Thus:

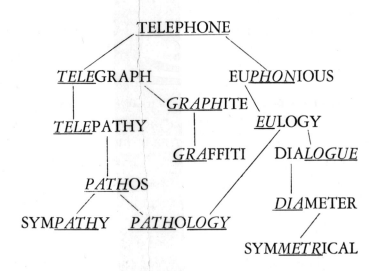

Now let's follow through on the calls to each of these italicized Greek combining forms and see how many useful English words we can get into our conversation.

TELE . . . far away

tele*phone*:   hearing *sound* from far away.

tele*graph*:   receiving *writing* from far away.

tele*pathy*:   receiving someone's thoughts or *feelings* from far away.

tele*scope*:   an instrument with which to see or *watch* something far away; a micro*scope* enables us to watch things so small (*micro*) that they cannot be seen with the naked eye.

tel*star*:   a recently coined word describing a man-made star which by reflection enables us to see things happening on the other side of the world.

| tele*vis*ion: | *seeing* from far off. This word is only half Greek. *Vision* comes from Latin via French. The root *vis* is seen in such words as *vis*ible, *vis*it (go to see), *vis*ta, *vis*ual, *vis*or (the part of the helmet that protected the eyes of knights in battle but through which they could nevertheless see). |

PHON, PHONO . . . sound

phono*graph*:	sound *writing*; an instrument that plays a record on which sound has been written (*graph*) or scratched in.
*eu*phonious:	*pleasant* (*eu*) sounding.
*caco*phonous:	(*caco*, bad) harsh sounding.
phon*ics*:	the science of sound, *ics* being a suffix used in names of many sciences and arts: eugen*ics*, athlet*ics*, ceram*ics*, statist*ics*, etc.
*mega*phone:	an instrument *enlarging* (*mega*, large, great) sound.

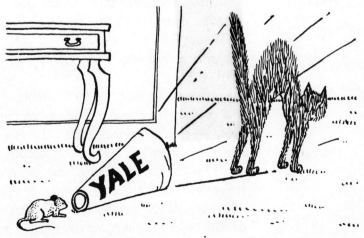

*sym*phony: a blending *together* (*sym*) of sounds, as in a full orchestra.

*xylo*phone: a musical instrument from which sounds are produced by striking strips of *wood* (*xylo*) of different lengths.

GRAPH . . . write

*lexico*grapher: writer of *lexicons* or dictionaries.

*carto*grapher: one who charts maps.

*photo*graphy: writing with *light* (*photo*), since it is the light let in through the opening in the camera that *writes* on the chemically treated film.

*ortho*graphy: *correct* (*ortho*) writing, a fancy word for correct spelling.

*calli*graphy: *beautiful* (*calli*) handwriting; *kaleido*-scope, an instrument through which we see a beautiful (here *kal* instead of *calli*) combination of colors in changing patterns.

*epi*graph: a suitable quotation that appears *above* (*epi*, on, above) a chapter, as in most of Sir Walter Scott's novels.

*steno*grapher: one who writes *shorthand* (*steno*—narrow).

*poly*graph: a lie detector because, to put it simply, it is a machine that makes tracings of the *many* (*poly*) variations of the pulse rate.

*holo*graph: something written *wholly* (*holo*, wholly, total) in the handwriting of the author. Recently in the library of Madrid, Spain, 700 pages of the notebooks of Leonardo da Vinci with drawings and descriptions in his own handwriting were discovered—a historic holographic find!

*holo*graphy: a newly-coined word for a new technique in photography using laser light waves, which promises to take the *whole* picture, making it three dimensional, for television and moving pictures—in short, *total* photography. Of course, the word should really be *holophotography*, but the root *photo* was somehow lost!

graphite: the part of the "lead" pencil that writes.

graffiti: (pronounced gra-fee-tee) an Italian word taken over into English, referring to the scribblings found occasionally on the walls of ancient caves and more frequently on the surfaces of modern walls.

Let us disconnect our telephone discussion for a moment. If I told you that the Greek root *caust* means fire (a *caustic* remark burns), would you be able to figure out what *holocaust* means in this world of hydrogen bombs? That's right: *total* destruction by *fire*. The word, however, is also used for any gigantic catastrophe or disaster. *Encaustic*, by the way, was the purple ink used by Roman emperors to "burn" their signatures *into* their decrees. Cut the word *encaustic* down to its first three letters, and you get our word *ink*! And so we've come full circle back to the word *writing*.

But let's plug into our switchboard again.

Path is a Greek root which, as the switchboard indicates, goes off in two directions: in one it means a strong

feeling sometimes associated with suffering; in the other
it means suffering that becomes disease.

PATH (1) . . . strong feeling

pathos: a strong feeling of sadness; a *pathetic*
                   creature is one you feel sorry for.

*a*pathy: no (*a*) strong feeling one way or another;
                   indifference; the *a* (or *an* before a vowel)
                   in front of Greek elements always says *no*
                   or *not*: *a*typical means not typical; *a*nony-
                   mous, nameless.

*anti*pathy: a strong feeling *against* (*anti*).

*sym*pathy: a strong feeling *with* (*sym*) someone in
                   his sorrow; *com*passion.

*em*pathy: different from sympathy in that you are
                   not *with*, you are *inside* (*em*); you feel as
                   deeply as the person suffering.

PATH (2) . . . disease

patho*logy*:   the study (*logy*) of disease.

patho*gen*ic: causing or giving *birth* to disease.

*psycho*pathic: relating to diseases of the *mind*.

EU . . . good, well, pleasant

eu*logy*:   *words* of praise; *speaking* well of someone.

eu*phem*ism: saying in a nice way something that is un-
                   pleasant or might seem offensive: for ex-
                   ample, many people would rather say, "He
                   passed away" than "He died." Or they say
                   "My goodness" to avoid the mention of
                   the Deity in some frivolous connection.

When diplomats announce that they have agreed "in
principle" it is usually a euphemism for "Nothing specific has been accomplished."

euphoria: a sense of well-being, of carrying things off well.

eugenics: the science that deals with improving the race of man; the name Eugene means well-born.

Enough? I think so. We'll disconnect our switch-board. But we won't leave ancient Greece. We can't. Our Defense Department has gone back to ancient Greek names—chiefly gods of Greek mythology—for the names of its missiles.

The Poseidon missile is named for the Greek god of earthquakes, water, and the sea (known as Neptune by the Romans). The Nike-Zeus antiballistic missile system comes from Nike, the Greek goddess of victory, and Zeus, the thunderbolt-wielding ruler of the Olympian deities, whom the Romans called Jupiter. In Jupiter we can see a blend of Zeus and pater—Zeus, the father of the gods.

So you see that if it's Greek to you, you may be able to understand many, many more words better.

And so you have begun your trip of exploration among words. Bon voyage!

INDEX OF WORDS